Mira Silverstein's
GUIDE TO
LOOPED AND
KNOTTED STITCHES

Books by Mira Silverstein include:

FUN WITH BARGELLO
FUN WITH APPLIQUÉ
BARGELLO PLUS
INTERNATIONAL NEEDLEWORK DESIGNS
MIRA SILVERSTEIN'S GUIDE TO UPRIGHT STITCHES
MIRA SILVERSTEIN'S GUIDE TO LOOPED AND KNOTTED STITCHES
MIRA SILVERSTEIN'S GUIDE TO SLANTED STITCHES
MIRA SILVERSTEIN'S GUIDE TO COMBINATION STITCHES

Mira Silverstein's

GUIDE TO LOOPED AND KNOTTED STITCHES

XXXXXXXXXXXXXXXXXXXXXXXXXXXXXXXXXXXXXXXXXXXXXXXXXXXX

Exciting Needlework Projects, Patterns,
and Designs **Anyone Can Make**

ARTWORK BY ROBERTA FRAUWIRTH

PHOTOGRAPHS BY SANDY L. STUDIOS

DAVID McKAY COMPANY, INC.
New York

I wish to take this opportunity to thank all those who worked with me in a professional capacity and especially Barbara Anderson who helped edit this book.

Samples finished by Ida Gold, Harriet Alonso, Carol B. Kempner, Mindi Kantor, Shirley Kantor, Elise Silverstein, Gigi Strauss, Joan Hyman, Mary McGregor, Eve Charny, Marie Gunther, and Jane Benson.

Diagrams on pages 25, 102, 103, and 104 by Shirley Rose.

Library of Congress Cataloging in Publication Data

Silverstein, Mira.
    Mira Silverstein's Guide to looped and knotted stitches.

    1. Needlework.   2. Embroidery.   I. Title.
II.   Title: Guide to looped and knotted stitches.
TT760.S5   746.4'4   77-11643
ISBN 0-679-50821-X
ISBN 0-679-50785-X pbk.

10 9 8 7 6 5 4 3 2

Manufactured in the United States of America

Designed by Jacques Chazaud

For Dean

XX

CONTENTS

INTRODUCTION   10

IMPORTANT INFORMATION FOR THE BEGINNER   12
    Threading the Needle and Anchoring Yarn   12
    Transferring Methods   13
    Fabric   15
    Yarns   21
    Tools and Supplies   22

LOOPED STITCHES   26
    Chain Stitch   26
    Magic Chain Stitch   29
    Lazy Daisy Stitch   30
    Buttonhole (Blanket) Stitch   32
    Feather Stitch   36
    Cretan Stitch   38
    Fly Stitch   40
    Vandyke Stitch   42
    Fishbone Stitch   44
    Shell (Sheaf Stitch Pattern)   46
    Rococo Stitch   50

KNOTTED STITCHES   55
    Turkish Knots   55
    Smyrna Knots   60
    French Knots   62
    Bullion Knots   64
    Beads and Sequins   67

PROJECTS   69
    Looped Flowers   69
    Red Rooster   74
    Rya Rugs   76
    Embroidered Buttons   78
    Card Boxes   80
    Chinese Butterflies and Flowers   86
    Pillow   87
    Scarf   87
    Brick Cover   92
    Embroidered Tunic   96
    Alphabet   98

FINISHING INSTRUCTIONS   101
    Blocking Textured Needlework   101
    Framing Needlework   101
    Mitering Fabric   103
    How to Make a Pillow   104

LIST OF SUPPLIERS   106

XX

INTRODUCTION

Needlework is the general term used to describe all work done with the threaded needle, both by hand and by machine. It is divided into two main categories: utilitarian needlework or sewing, where stitches perform the basic function of joining fabrics; and decorative needlework, where stitches are used to create a design which decorates the fabric surface and becomes part of the fabric itself.

There are various kinds of decorative needlework. The most familiar are listed below.

Embroidery is a term most often used to describe decorative needlework applied to fine, densely woven fabrics, such as linen, silk, or cotton.

Crewel is embroidery worked with wool yarn or yarns of similar textures on compatible fabrics, such as linen or wool.

Canvas work refers to the kind of fabric used and not a special kind of needlework. Canvas is an open-mesh, even-weave fabric and the stitches worked on it will be a little more "patterned," or uniform, than those worked on denser cloth.

Counted-thread indicates the manner of workmanship when the design is not painted on the fabric but is reproduced from a graphed outline. The graph is counted in stitches or stitch units, and the fabric is counted in threads. The more threads alloted to a stitch unit, the larger the gauge of the design.

Surface embroidery is a figure of speech since all embroidery is worked on the surface.

Needlepoint is sometimes used to describe canvas work in general and the Half-cross or Continental stitch in particular. However, it is not a stitch. It is only another term for work with a threaded needle, or "point of the needle."

Creative stitchery refers to the most artist form of needlework when the stitches are used to create an original design on the fabric rather than first painting the design on the fabric and then filling it in with stitches. Creative stitchery is also a general term for embroidery or stitchery. It is the art or craft of decorating fabric with lines and loops in interesting patterns with the aid of a threaded needle. The lines and loops are known as stitches.

The basic, or line, stitch is a straight line between two points and is executed with a threaded needle. The threaded needle is brought to the surface of the fabric, carried across it in a predetermined direction, then brought back to the reverse side of the fabric to complete the stitch.

A line stitch cannot curve or flex by itself unless it is anchored in some way by another stitch. The line stitch must therefore be manipulated to create a shape other than a straight line on the face of the fabric. All the knotted, looped, and tied stitches are the result of this manipulation. These stitches are very flexible and may be used on any fabric as long as the yarns and needles are compatible. The looped, tied, and knotted stitches introduced here are the easiest to learn and can be used in many ways. With the exception of the Shell Stitch pattern, these stitches are not geometric and do not require counted-thread fabric. However, they are shown on open-mesh diagrams and in stitch detail to make their construction easier to understand.

When a number of line stitches are worked side by side, crossed over, or placed in any combination to form a specific pattern, they create what is called a stitch formation, or stitch pattern.

Each stitch formation has its own distinctive texture when worked over a large area. This texture is immediately altered with the slightest adjustment in the length and number of lines in the individual stitch pattern.

There are hundreds of stitch patterns in the lexicon of needlework. They are often identified by name and place of origin. Most of them are minor variations of a handful of classic patterns.

This is a beginners' introduction to basic decorative needlework. The accent is on the construction of stitches and stitch patterns that, once mastered, will enable the beginner to create a wide variety of beautiful and useful projects. Each stitch and stitch pattern will be outlined in step-by-step detail, and its special properties and usage will be explained. Many design projects are introduced in this book. However, beginners are encouraged to further diversify and explore, to invent new stitch patterns, to create unusual color combinations, and to alter, adapt, or adjust. The possibilities are endless.

XX

IMPORTANT INFORMATION FOR THE BEGINNER

Threading the Needle and Anchoring Yarn

For those who have never worked with canvas and yarn, a little practice is recommended before embarking on a large project. The best way to learn anything is by doing.

Read the sections on materials and supplies and buy a small piece of firm, interlocked # 12 canvas, a few small skeins of Persian-type yarn in assorted colors, and a blunt-pointed needle.

Cut the canvas into small easy-to-handle pieces, and cover the edges with paper or plastic tape. (Surgical and cellophane tapes will not adhere properly to canvas.) Even if the canvas does not ravel, the edges are rough and should be taped.

To thread the needle, fold the end of a strand of yarn over the needle and hold both firmly between thumb and forefinger. Pull the needle away without disturbing the yarn fold. Press the fold between the fingers until yarn is flat and barely visible. Press the eye of the tapestry needle over this fold and don't release the yarn until the needle is threaded.

To begin work on a bare canvas, pull the threaded needle up through the fabric, leaving a tail of about 2" on the reverse side. Hold this tail down with one hand while you work the first few stitches over it, catching some of the yarn in the process.

Subsequent strands should be slipped through a worked area and held in place for the first stitch or two. Don't use knots in canvas work—they can almost always be detected. If a knot comes undone, there probably won't be enough yarn to reanchor it, and several stitches may have to be taken out and replaced.

To end off the yarn, slide it into a worked area and keep all visible tails clipped. Tails will tangle the working yarn and the wool will shed a fuzz which will carry onto the right side of the work and become imbedded in the stitches.

Transferring Methods

Before a design can be embroidered, it must first be transferred onto the chosen fabric. There are a number of transferring methods that employ one or more steps of the standard three-step procedure: altering dimension; tracing; and transferring. The method depends on the fabric and type of embroidery to be done.

Altering the dimension involves enlarging or reducing the design. Generally speaking, the design outlines illustrated in books or magazines are reduced in size to save space. A design can be enlarged or reduced by making a photostat. This involves an inexpensive photo enlarging process that is fast and accurate.

Check with local newspapers or printing shops for the photostat service nearest you. A photostat is *not* the same as a photocopy. Photocopy machines, available in most libraries and some general stores, will duplicate a sheet of paper no larger than legal size. A Xerox duplicating machine will offer the same service.

If a design is divided over several pages, photocopy (or photostat if an enlargement is desired) each page and assemble the parts with tape. Before enlarging, check the design carefully for any changes you may wish to make. Obliterate unwanted portions with white poster paint, and draw any additions with a black felt-tip marking pen.

The alterntive to making a photostat is the old square-by-square method of enlarging. Draw a margin all around the design (if there isn't one already) and divide the area into sixteen equal squares or rectangles. Do this by measuring and dividing the pattern in half and then in quarters, both vertically and horizontally. Take a sheet of paper the size of the desired enlargement, outline the margin, and divide it into the same number of squares or rectangles as the original pattern. For a complicated design, subdivide the squares into thirty-two smaller ones. Number the squares in sequence on both the design and the enlargement papers and proceed to copy the design square-for-square. The accuracy of the enlargement will depend on individual artistic ability. Remember to make all necessary alterations at this time.

A design may be reduced in size in the same manner that it is enlarged. Make all changes *after* the reduction is completed.

When the tracing method of transferring is used, a photostat or an enlarged drawing becomes the master copy. The design must now be copied onto tracing paper, a semi-sheer paper available in art supplies stores. It comes in rolls or pads of assorted sizes. If necessary, tape several sheets together with cellophane tape. Place tape-side down on the enlargement, and trace the design outline very carefully with a soft black pencil. Trace on a smooth hard surface, and fasten both papers wilh push pins to prevent shifting.

The tracing is the working copy, which is used in the final step of design transfer. Press the selected fabric, and then tape it to a smooth flat surface. Place a sheet of dressmakers carbon (transfer paper) shiny-side *down* over the fabric, and position the tracing on top so it is properly centered. Place a few push pins all around, and go over the design outline with a hard pencil. Press firmly to get a clear sharp outline on the fabric.

Transfer paper is sold in dressmaker supplies stores, and it comes in light or dark colors. Do not use typewriter carbon.

Note: If the fabric is too large to be taped down, use paper-weights, heavy books, or felt-covered bricks in several places to keep it flat. If the design has to fit into a special framework and the opaque transfer paper interferes with proper placement, position the tracing and pin it to the fabric on one side. Lift the other side and slide in the transfer paper.

Pre-test transfer paper on a scrap of fabric to make sure the outlines are clear and sharp. Constant lifting and checking as you trace the design may cause the outline to shift.

If your fabric is sheer enough, you can save time by tracing the design directly onto the fabric. Tape the design to a flat surface and place the sheer fabric over it. Fasten with a few push pins, and trace with a fine indelible or smudge-proof pen. Needlepoint canvas will lie flat, but sheer fabrics, such as organdy, tend to shift and must be secured with extra care. This method will not work on textured fabrics with a deep pile because they are not sheer enough to see through.

To transfer a design onto heavier, more textured fabrics, place the fabric on a frame or embroidery hoop (see page 23). Pin or baste the tracing onto the fabric, and stitch the main design outlines through the paper. Peel away the paper and go over the outlines if necessary. Then fill in the rest of the stitches. Or work the entire design through the paper. If the fabric is washable, the paper will disintegrate when washed; otherwise, remove what paper is visible and leave the rest. It will not harm the embroidery.

A tracing can be turned into a hot-iron transfer by outlining it with a Hectograph pencil (see List of Suppliers). This is a pink wax pencil that may be sharpened like an ordinary pencil and gives a clear sharp outline. Turn the tracing right-side down and retrace the entire outline with the Hectograph. Then turn the tracing right-side up, position it onto the fabric, and glide a hot iron over the paper. The resulting outline will be sharp and clear. This method *must* be pre-tested on a small piece of fabric. The temperature of the iron is most important: if it is too cool, the transfer will be unclear; if it is too hot, the outline will smudge. Be careful —an iron that is hot enough to transfer Hectograph may scorch certain fabrics.

If you have the right combination of fabric and temperature, the Hectograph marks are easily removed by dry cleaning, or they can be washed out with soap and water.

Fabric

Needlepoint canvas is the most familiar of the background fabrics. It is an even-weave cotton fabric with open meshes that are easy to count. There are two basic types of canvas: single-thread, or mono; and double-thread, or Penelope.

Mesh is another word for canvas thread, and the gauge is the number of meshes per inch. A canvas with twelve threads per inch is sold as # 12 mesh. The more meshes to the inch, the smaller the stitches.

Canvas is available in a large number of gauges, but the ones most suitable for beginners are # 10 or # 12. Canvas with a gauge larger than # 5 should be double-thread because single threads will not support the heavy yarn needed to cover it.

FIGURE 1

A., # 12 Mono canvas (interwoven) in tan; B, # 5 Double thread canvas in white (suitable for rugs); C, # 12 Mono canvas (interlocked); D, # 10 Mono canvas (interwoven) with raveled threads. Finished edges are called selvedge.

16

Mono canvas is a simple weave of single vertical and horizontal threads. (Figure 1, A and D.) It comes in stark white as well as a variety of colors, and its smooth, flat surface is ideal for tracing and painting designs. Mono canvas is best suited for the straight Gobelin or Bargello needlework. It is a standard, loosely interwoven fabric with durable threads that can withstand a great deal of wear and tear. It is recommended for large projects, especially those that will be used for upholstery.

There is a new interlocked mono canvas (Figure 1, C) which features smooth flat threads that do not unravel easily. It is an excellent choice for small projects. However, the interlocked canvas is not recommended for needlework that requires extensive blocking because the lightweight threads tend to break when stretched.

Double-thread, or Penelope, canvas is the heaviest of all canvases and is excellent for heavy looped work, such as Turkish knots. It is available in widths up to 60" in white, beige, or yellow. (Figure 1, B.)

A canvas of good quality is firm but not rigid. The mesh threads run straight and true, and the knots that re-tie broken threads are far apart and barely visible.

Freshly unrolled canvas may seem a little crooked, but a good tug at opposite corners should straighten it out. A very firm canvas that resists the tug may be relaxed by giving it a light steaming and then pulling it back into shape before it dries and regains its firmness.

Needlepoint canvas is always coated with a special starch called sizing. This gives it body and a firm support for stitches. An open-mesh cotton fabric would otherwise be limp, and the mesh threads would lose their form under the pressure of the heavy yarns. The stitches would look uneven and the over-all effect would be unattractive.

Starched, or sized, fabric is essential for all work that will require blocking. In the blocking process, a distorted canvas is pulled back into shape and nailed to a board. The sizing is softened by steaming. As it dries, it regains its firmness as well as its original shape. (For more information, see the chapter on blocking.)

FIGURE 2

Clockwise: Even-weave Linen;
Embroidery Linen;
Rya Cloth;
Aida Even-weave Cotton;
Linda Fine Even-weave Cotton

Linen (Figure 2, A and B) is an old standby of embroidery fabrics. It comes in a large range of textures, widths, and qualities, and it creates a beautiful background.

Aida (Figure 2, D) is a fine even-weave cotton fabric that resembles monk's cloth. It is available in a variety of colors and gauges and is excellent for counted-stitch work as well as for embroidery.

Linda (Figure 2, E) is a very fine even-weave cotton cloth that is less costly than linen. It comes in over two dozen fresh colors and in 42" width.

Rya cloth (Figure 2, C) is a specially woven fabric for Rya or Turkish knots. Open mesh and closely woven rows alternate to create even spacing between the rows of loops. Rya is a durable fabric and makes an excellent background for the heaviest looped rugs. It comes in 36" width and in gray only.

The above fabrics may be purchased at most needlework shops, or see the List of Suppliers on page 106.

Lace can best be described as fancy open-work fabric. It makes an interesting background for free-style embroidery. Lace is sold by the yard and comes in a large selection of patterns, colors, and widths.

Narrow strips of lace may be joined to make larger pieces of fabric for curtains, tablecloths, placemats, and other decorative accessories. When making any of these items, however, it is very difficult to work with the lace alone. Outline the pattern on a sheet of strong pliable paper, such as parchment or tracing paper, and then pin the pieces of lace to this paper pattern, making sure to overlap the edges of the lace. Handle the lace lightly to avoid stretching it. Pin, baste, and then machine stitch the lace right through the paper. When all edges have been sewn, simply peel away the paper.

Simple articles of clothing such as blouses and caftans can also be made from lace. Once again, the lace should be attached to a paper pattern of the item you wish to make. Overlap and stitch the lace edging, and then peel away the paper. The cut edges of seams on lace garments are folded back and stitched like any cloth garments.

Lace is sometimes over-embroidered. To avoid a cluttered look,

FIGURE 3

select a design within the lace fabric itself and go over it with Chain or Buttonhole stitches or work a simple running stitch in and and out of the lace openings. Use assorted colors in polished cotton-silk or rayon embroidery threads. (Figure 3.)

Yarns

Needlepoint yarns come in a wide variety of colors and textures. The yarns used in canvas work must be strong enough to withstand the pull through the canvas without fraying.

Persian yarn is the most popular and practical needlepoint yarn. It is all wool and is available in an enormous selection of colors. Persian yarn is made of three strands (plies), which separate easily and may be adapted to any size mesh by adding or removing one or more plies. Subtle shadings can be achieved by blending two or more shades.

English crewel is also a multi-ply wool yarn. It is somewhat thinner than the Persian type and may require an extra strand of yarn to cover a given canvas.

Tapestry yarn is a four-ply twist that does not separate into single plies. It is excellent for any needlework but only fits some canvas gauges, usually # 10 and sometimes # 12. Pre-test on a piece of canvas before beginning a large project.

Silk is one of the most beautiful needlepoint materials. The English silk is a little more shiny than the French, and it has a tendency to fray. French silk has a beautiful satin luster and is very nice to work with. Add small amounts of silk for highlights and a touch of elegance.

Six-strand emboridery floss is a soft and manageable cotton thread that comes in many colors and may be used to highlight small areas. It soils easily and should not be worked over a large area, unless the needlework is washable.

There are a number of needlepoint yarns made from synthetic fibers. They do not come in as many colors as wool yarns, and they have a tendency to mat after a time. However, they are washable, non-allergic, and often less expensive than wool.

Renewing Yarn Texture

Yarn may become matted for a number of reasons. The strands look fuzzy and they seem to stick together. When this occurs, soak the yarn in Woolite and cool water for a few minutes and then squeeze the moisture out by running your fingers along the strands. Let dry over a towel.

Tools and Supplies

Needles. Needles come in a large variety of specialized shapes and sizes. They are divided into two general categories: sharp-pointed, such as crewel and darners for work on densely woven fabrics, and blunt-pointed (tapestry) needles for open weaves such as canvas or net. Needles must be compatible with both the fabric and the working yarns. Purchase them by size (gauge). The finer the needle the larger its number. Needles are distributed under different brand names, and although the eye gauge is fairly constant, the length of the shaft may vary. Find the length that is most comfortable in your hand.

In looped and knotted projects, the type of fabric used will determine the type of needle to be used. When working on an open-mesh canvas or executing special stitches, such as the Rococo, Shell, or Vandyke, a blunt-pointed (tapestry) needle should be used to avoid splitting the canvas threads. The eye of the tapestry needle should be large enough to allow the yarn to be easily threaded, and the shaft should be thin enough to slip through the canvas. When working on densely woven fabrics, a sharp-pointed (crewel) needle should be used. Crewel needles have large eyes, which can accommodate the heavier embroidery threads.

Thimbles. Thimbles are a matter of personal preference. Some needles slide through canvas so easily that it is not always necessary to use a thimble. But if you use one, select one that fits comfortably.

Scissors. Two pairs of scissors are a must: one small, sharp-pointed pair that fits into small areas to rip stitches or to cut yarn ends; and a large pair to cut canvas and other fabric.

Tape. Tape is another necessity. It should be the self-adhesive masking tape available in hardware stores. A 1" width is adequate. Fold it over the cut edge of the canvas to prevent the threads from raveling and to make the canvas easier to handle.

A **ruler** or measuring tape should also be part of your needlework "tool box," as well as some fine-point acrylic **marking pens**, and a small **magnet** to pick up stray pins and needles.

Hoops and Frames. A frame or hoop can be very useful in learning to work a variety of embroidery stitches. It is, of course, possible to work without a frame, but the number of stitches you can work would then be reduced. The main function of an embroidery frame or hoop is to stretch the fabric and keep it taut while working the stitches. Stitches worked on a frame look more even and require less blocking.

There is a large selection of hoops and frames available wherever needlepoint supplies are sold. (Figure 4.) The hoops are either round or oval, and the frames are rectangular with adjustable sides. The best ones can be anchored to a stand leaving both hands free.

The round hoops that fasten to a simple floor stand are excellent for small projects. The stands adjust to different heights, and the hoops are interchangeable. Therefore, you can leave a piece of work on one hoop while trying out some stitches on another. Some hoops screw onto a tabletop, and others are attached to a small platform one can sit on.

Round (hoop) frames come in two parts; one seamless ring fits inside a larger one that adjusts with a special screw. To mount the fabric onto a round hoop, adjust the screw on the outer ring so that it fits tightly over the inner ring and the fabric. Pull the fabric all around until it is taut. Then push the outer ring down. To release the fabric, press both thumbs on the fabric at the edge of the frame while lifting the outer ring.

Square frames are ideal for larger pieces of work. The width is usually standard from 18" to 36" but the length is adjusted on rollers at both ends. The rollers have strips of tape stapled across them. The side of the fabric that does not exceed the length of the strip is sewn to the tape at both ends. If the fabric is longer than the distance between the rollers, wind the surplus neatly over one roller. Lace the sides as shown in Figure E. If the sides of the needlepoint fabric do not have a heavy-duty selvage, stitch a length of tape or special stitch-webbing at either side before lacing.

When the embroidery on this portion of fabric is completed, the lacing is removed, the finished embroidery is rolled up at one end, and fresh fabric is unrolled at the other end. The sides are then laced again.

On any frame, the stitches should be worked in a two-step, up-and-down motion, not in a sewing motion. Always keep one hand below the frame and the other hand above. Each hand receives the needle as it is pushed by the other hand through the fabric. It takes a little practice, but the technique is simple once mastered.

When learning the stitch construction, especially of looped and knotted stitches, work in "slow motion" so that each step is clearly defined and notice when and how the yarn is looped around the needle. This will make it easier to work on a frame.

Note: Never crowd the embroidery inside the frame. Allow at least a 2" space between the embroidery outline and the frame-work.

FIGURE 4

A, Floor stand with hoop frame; B, Mounting fabric into a round hoop frame; C, Proper hand position when working with embroidery frame; D, Hoop frame with seamless ring inside larger ring with screw; E, Square frame with laced sides.

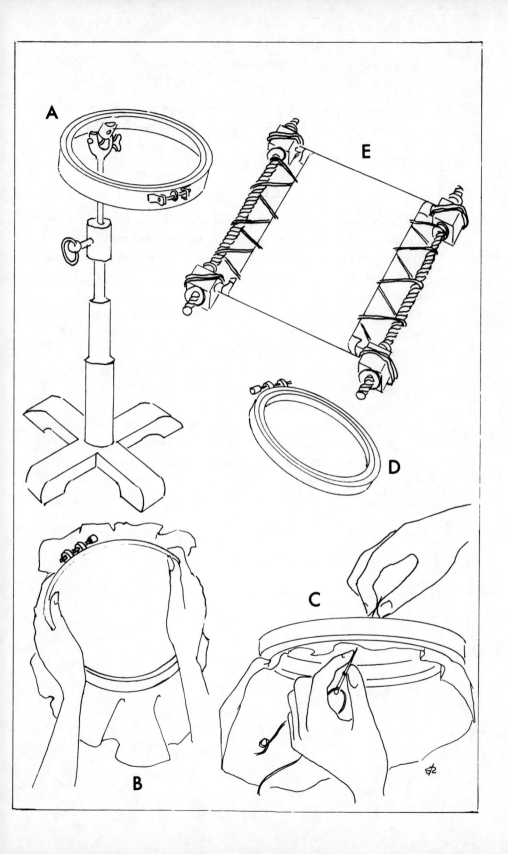

XX

LOOPED STITCHES

Chain Stitch

The Chain Stitch is one of the most ancient and versatile of embroidery stitches. It creates beautiful outlines and may be used to fill open areas. It can be worked with more than one color threaded in the same needle, and it is the basic stitch for the popular Lazy Daisy.

The Chain Stitch is shown on open-mesh canvas to illustrate its stitch construction. (Figure 5.) Actually it is used more frequently on densely woven embroidery fabrics.

Bring threaded needle out at 1, curve the yarn slightly, and bring the needle back into 1, out at 2, and over the looped yarn. Pull yarn gently to avoid distorting the curve of the stitch.

Repeat one stitch at a time, always inserting the needle inside the last loop. Work Chain Stitches as evenly as possible in straight and in curvilinear outlines. To fill an area with Chain Stitches, work the lines of stitches in the same direction. The stitches should be in close formation but not overcrowded. (Figure 6.)

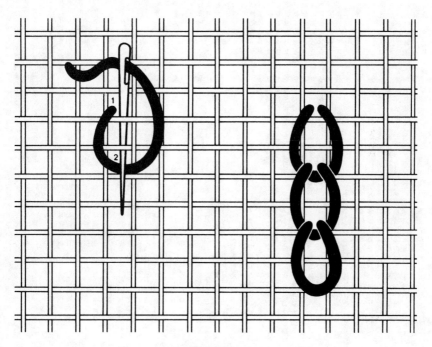

FIGURE 5
Chain Stitch Detail

Magic Chain Stitch

Thread two contrasting colors in one needle. Begin the first stitch as in Figure 5. Form a loop with both colors below the first stitch. Keep the darker thread under the needle and the lighter one above. As you pull the threads, the darker color will form a stitch and the lighter one will disappear on the reverse side. Repeat, this time changing the color sequence. The stitches will alternate colors. Work one dark and one light, or two dark and two light, or in any combination. (Figure 7.)

FIGURE 7
Magic Chain Stitch

FIGURE 6
Chain Stitch

29

Lazy Daisy Stitch

The Lazy Daisy consists of single chain loops worked in clusters of five or six. They are worked from the center, one loop at a time. The centers may be filled with one or more French knots.

Lazy Daisies are used for decorative borders or over-all patterns in random sizes. To create a fuller Lazy Daisy, make a second, smaller loop in the center of the first one. Single loops may be worked side-by-side for a narrow border. These are called Detached Chain Stitches. (Figures 8 and 9.)

FIGURE 8
Detached Chain Stitches

FIGURE 9
Lazy Daisy Stitch Detail

Buttonhole (Blanket) Stitch

The Buttonhole is one of the most versatile of the looped stitches. It may be worked in close formation or widely spaced (Blanket Stitch), in scallops or in circles. (Figure 10.)

Work the Buttonhole Stitch from left to right. Bring the threaded needle out at 1, go in at 2 and out at 3, looping the yarn under the needle. Finish off a strand of yarn at 2 and begin a fresh strand at 3. This will keep the row of loops unbroken.

The stitches are shown on canvas for easy visibility (Figure 11), but they are usually worked on densely woven fabrics. Learn to work the Buttonhole Stitch in nice even rows and make a Victorian box from old photographs (see page 80).

Even rows of Buttonhole Stitches may be used to create interesting geometric designs and to reproduce counted stitch patterns (see Figures 12 and 13, and the red rooster on color page 2).

FIGURE 11
Buttonhole Stitch

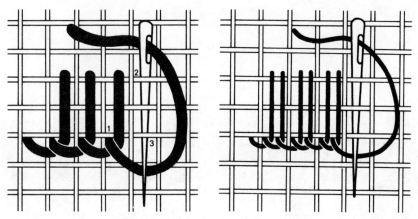

FIGURE 10 Buttonhole Stitch Detail

FIGURE 12
Geometric Design worked in Buttonhole Stitch

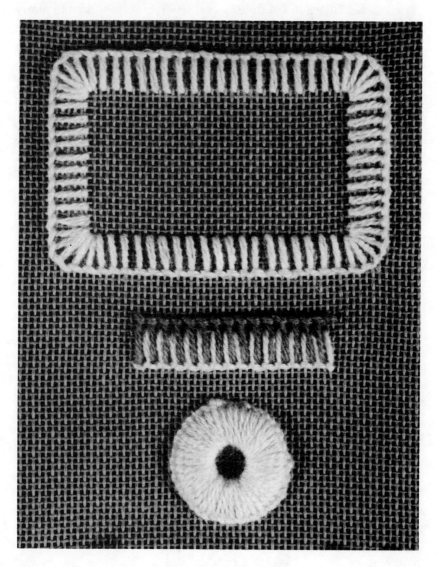

FIGURE 13

Feather Stitch

The Feather Stitch is a simple looped stitch that is worked in many different ways. It is used in crewel stitchery and in decorative overembroidery on quilts. This stitch is especially effective when it joins the irregular patches of a crazy quilt. (Figure 14.)

Bring threaded needle up at 1, down at 2, and up again at 3. Continue working the loops to the left and to the right, coming up at odd numbers and going back in at even numbers.

The Double Feather Stitch and the Closed Feather Stitch are only two of the many variations possible. The Double Feather is worked with two loops to the left and two to the right. (Figure 15.)

FIGURE 14
Feather Stitch Detail

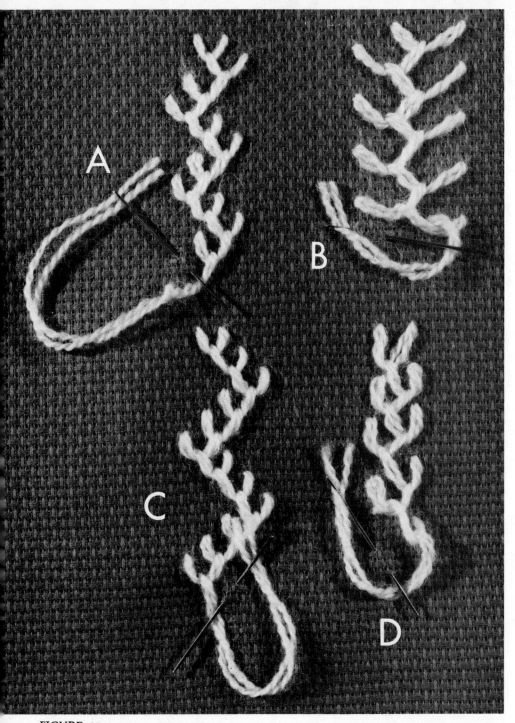

FIGURE 15

A, Double Feather Stitch; B, Single wide-open Feather Stitch; C, Triple Feather Stitch; D, Single closed Feather Stitch.

Cretan Stitch

The Cretan resembles the feather stitch. It is most often used to fill in leaf shapes in crewel stitchery. It may be worked tightly as a solid filler or fairly open to allow some fabric to show through. (Figure 16.)

Begin at the top and work the single stitch, coming up at 1, and going in at 2. Come up at 3, go in at 4, and come back up at 5 (below 2). Continue forming the loops to the left and to the right. The loops may fan out or taper in to shape a leaf, and a plaited line is formed in the center. (Figure 17.) Practice the Cretan Stitch on open-mesh canvas, and then work it on closely woven fabric.

FIGURE 17
Cretan Stitch

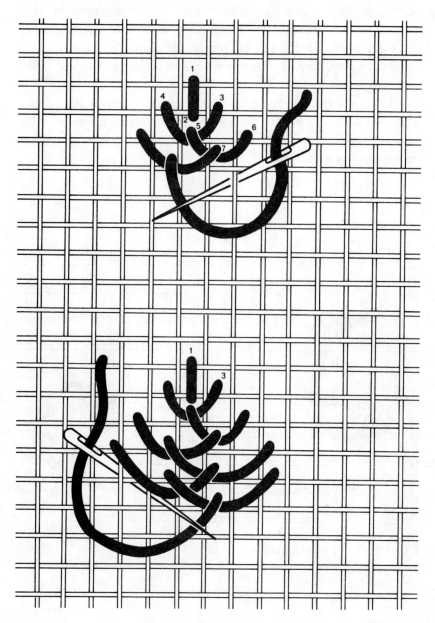

FIGURE 16
Cretan Stitch Detail

Fly Stitch

Although the Fly Stitch may be worked in vertical rows in close formation, it is generally worked in individual units scattered over the surface of the fabric. To create additional texture, the Fly Stitch can be placed at intervals over a background worked in the continental stitch.

Bring threaded needle up at 1 and go in at 2, leaving a loop. Come up at 3, and anchor the loop with one stitch taken over one canvas thread at 4. To repeat, come out directly below 1 or space the stitches as indicated in Figure 19.

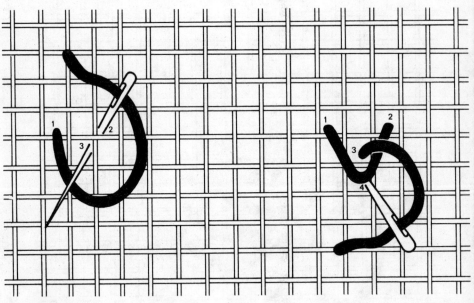

FIGURE 18   Fly Stitch Detail

FIGURE 19
Fly Stitch

Vandyke Stitch

The Vandyke is an anchored stitch that is used effectively in leaf shapes. It resembles the Cretan stitch because of the plait down the center, but it is worked differently. (Figure 20.)

The threaded needle comes up at 1, goes in at 2, comes up at 3, and goes back in at 4 to form the first cross at the top of the stitch pattern. From this point, the needle comes up at 5 and is slipped *under* the cross above wihout going into the fabric. It then goes in at 6, which is above 4. Continue working from lower left, under the cross and into the lower right. Work within an outline, keeping the edges even so that they will not require an additional outline.

The Vandyke Stitch is ideal for border outlines and may be worked in close formation or with spaces between the stitches. (Figure 21 shows an interesting variation of the Vandyke Stitch.)

Note: Work with a blunt needle which will not catch the yarns as it slips under the cross.

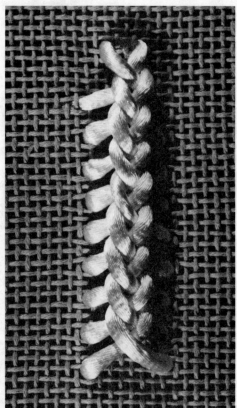

FIGURE 21
Vandyke Stitch

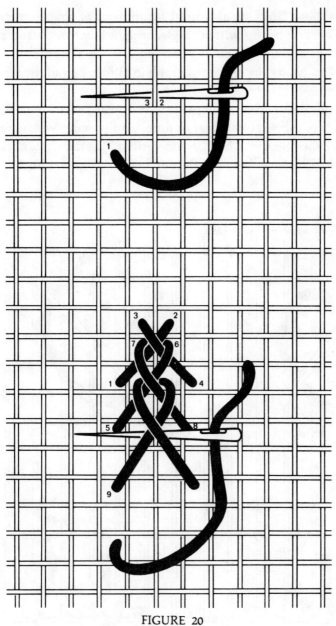

FIGURE 20
Vandyke Stitch Detail

Fishbone Stitch

The Fishbone Stitch is also used for filling leaf shapes in crewel embroidery. It begins with a single straight stitch at the top and is worked in a series of loops anchored like the fly stitch in close formation. Study the four-step graph in Figure 22 and the samples in Figure 23.

Practice the Fishbone on open-mesh canvas and then work it on embroidery fabric. Draw leaf outlines and practice widening and tapering the stitches. The Fishbone Stitch, like the Cretan, can be worked with spaces between the stitches for a lighter effect.

FIGURE 22 Fishbone Stitch Detail

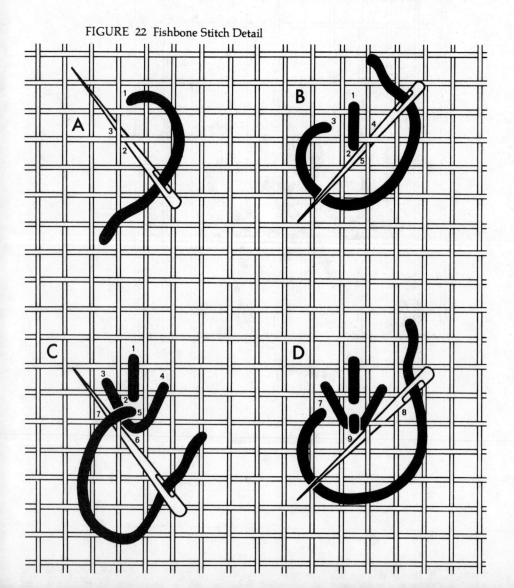

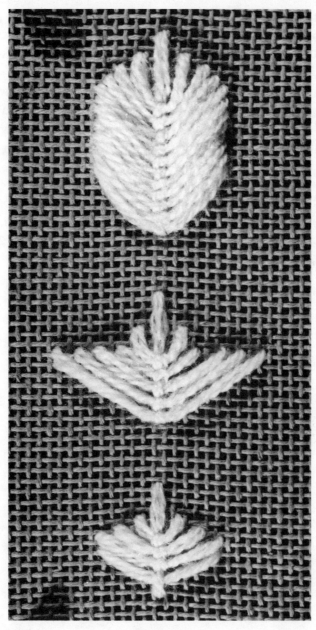

FIGURE 23
Fishbone Stitch

Shell (Sheaf) Stitch Pattern

To create the Shell Stitch Pattern, the needle comes out at 1, goes in at 2, out at 3, in at 4, out at 5, in at 6, out at 7, and in at 8. Bring the needle out at 9, which is the same line as the 5-6 stitch between the third and fourth canvas threads. Push the stitches to the left with your finger in order to slip the needle through easily without catching it in the yarn. Carry yarn across to the right and insert the needle at 10, which is on the same line as the 3-4 stitch. Pull yarn just enough to gather the four stitches into a sheaf. (Figure 24.)

This is a large decorative stitch. The open diamond spaces may be filled in with large French knots or any number of small stitches in matching or contrasting colors. A shiny thread may be woven in and out of the horizontal tie stitches. (Figures 25 and 26.)

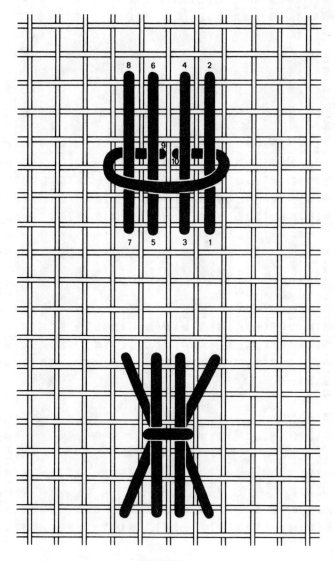

FIGURE 24
Sheaf Stitch Detail

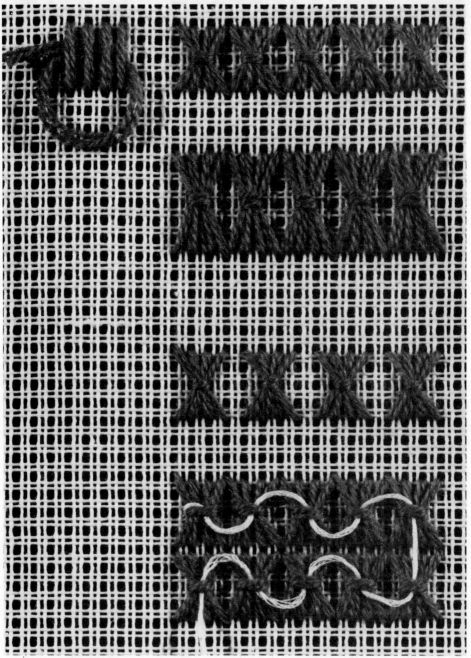

FIGURE 25
Sheaf Stitch

FIGURE 26
Sheaf Stitch Texture

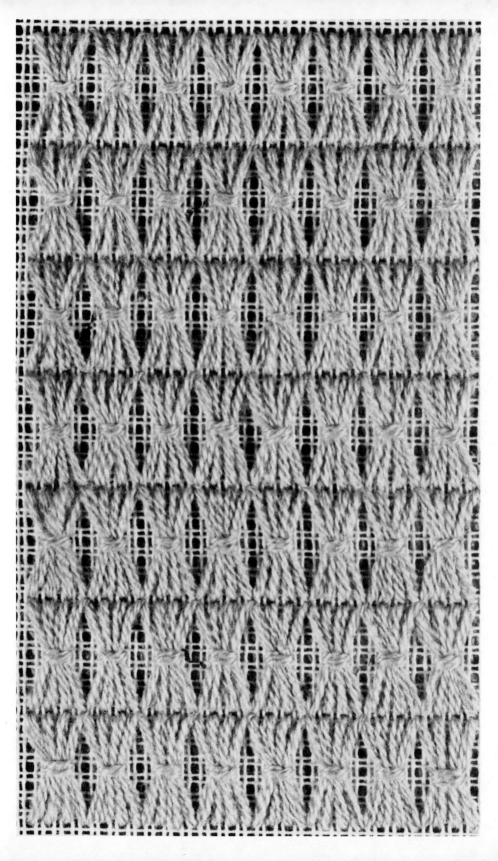

Rococo Stitch

The Rococo is a handsome, textured stitch that may be worked in bold yarns on heavy fabrics as well as in fine threads on lightweight fabrics. Begin by working on mono canvas in order to understand the construction of this stitch pattern. (Figure 27.)

Force open the canvas at 1 and 2 by twisting a closed pair of embroidery scissors into the canvas hole, being careful not to break the threads. Bring the threaded needle out at 1, come in at 2, and go out at 3. Pull thread tightly and place a small stitch across the long vertical 1-2. To do this, go in at 4 and out at 1 as in Figure B. Follow steps in Figure 5 C, D, and E. The long vertical stitches all go in at 1 and out at 2, but they are spaced one canvas thread apart as they are anchored with the small horizontal stitches and pulled into a curved line.

After making the first three stitches to the left, repeat by working three stitches curving to the right. This completes one stitch unit.

Begin the second stitch unit at the arrow point in Figure 28. Always force the canvas open before beginning the stitch unit, pulling tightly so that the openings are visible, and complete one stitch unit before going on to the next one. Avoid crossing the working thread behind the holes. These openings give the work a lacy effect. Figures 29 and 30 show samples worked in the Rococo Stitch.

Rococo Stitches have a natural scalloped edge that may be used as part of the design. Line the finished piece with dark fabric to emphasize the effect of the open work.

FIGURE 27
Rococo Stitch Detail

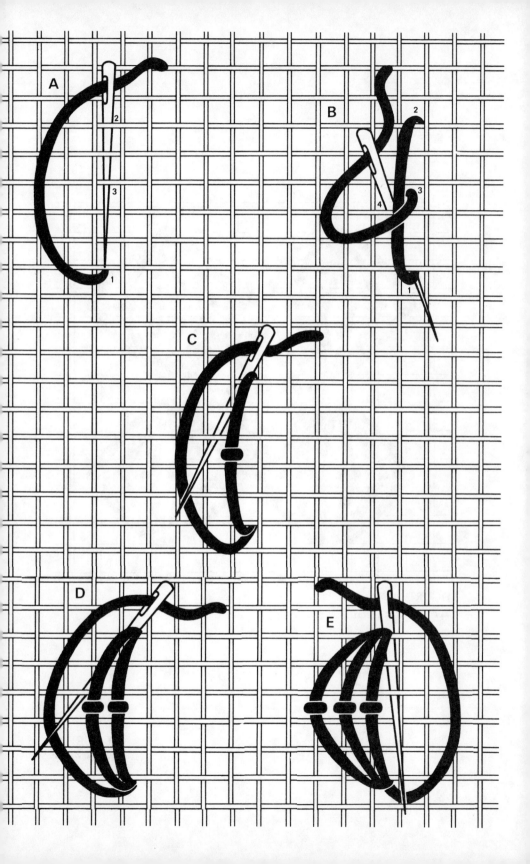

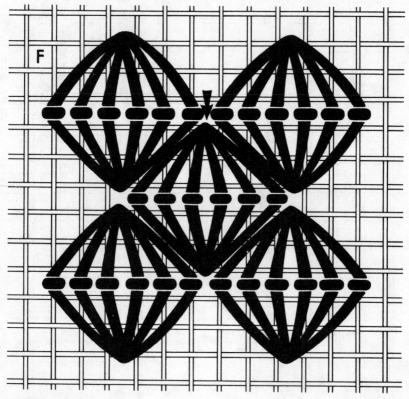

FIGURE 28
Rococo Stitch Detail

FIGURE 29
Rococo Stitch

52

FIGURE 30

KNOTTED STITCHES

Turkish Knots

The Turkish Knot is a very useful stitch and well worth learning to work correctly. Two versions are shown in Figures 31 and 32. In the first version, the needle comes in under one vertical canvas thread. The yarn tail stays on the top side of the canvas. The threaded needle comes in at 1 and out at 2, then over to the right, in at 3, and out at 4. As in Figure B, place your left thumb over the yarn loop at X and bring the needle in again at 1 and 2. Repeat the stitches in close formation as in Figure C. Pull the knots tightly. The length of the loops is determined by eye, and after some practice you will learn to work them in fairly even rows.

In the second version of the Turkish Knot, the needle comes in at an angle under the crossover point of the canvas threads. The loop is slightly different from the first version, and there is a thread of canvas showing under the horizontal stitch that holds the loop. However, on a large piece of work the difference hardly matters.

Practice both versions and adopt the one you like best. Always work Turkish Knots from the bottom line up and from left to right. Long loops and heavy rug yarns may be spaced with two or three rows of canvas left unworked. It depends on the gauge of the canvas and the weight of the yarn.

Turkish Knots may be left long and uncut, or they may be partially cut, shag cut, or velvet cut. (Figures 33 and 34.) They may be worked on any embroidery fabric but look best on even-weave fabric. The heavy double-mesh canvas and Rya cloth are excellent for rugs worked in Turkish Knots.

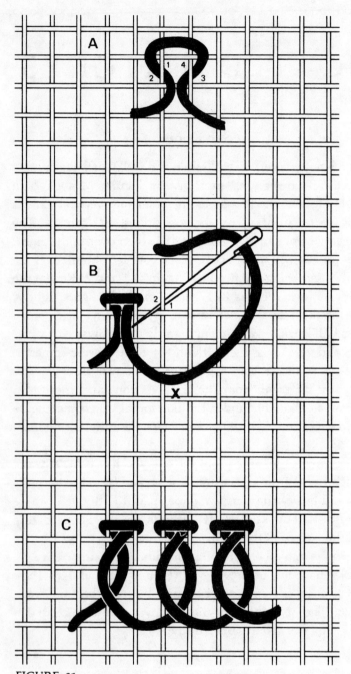

FIGURE 31
Turkish Knot Stitch Detail (Version # 1)

FIGURE 32
Turkish Knot Stitch Detail (Version # 2)

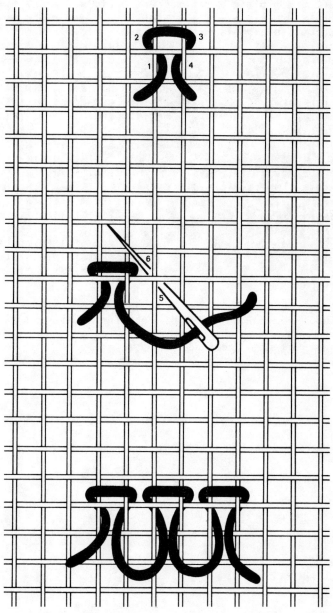

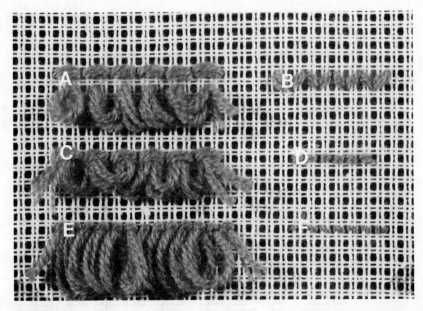

FIGURE 33

A, Turkish Knot Stitch (Version# 2), right side; B, Version # 2, underside; C, Turkish Knot Stitch (Version # 1) right side worked over double threads; D, Version # 1, underside; E, Version# 1 worked over single canvas threads; F, Version# 1, single thread underside.

FIGURE 34

Turkish Knots finished a number of ways: A, Velvet-cut; B, Uncut; C, Partially cut; D, Random cut or shag.

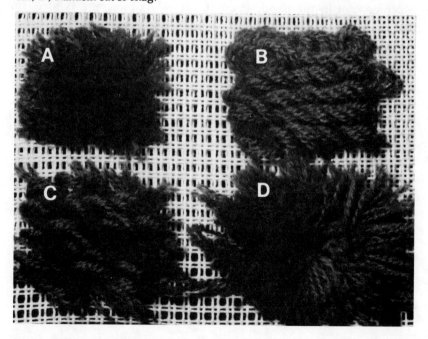

Smyrna Knots

The Smyrna Knot is slightly different in construction from the Turkish knot. It is used when an even pile is desired. It works best with a gauge stick. This is a flat stick which you can make in wood or heavy cardboard. Its width determines the stitch gauge. (Figure 35.)

Anchor the first stitch with a small knot (Figures A and B in diagram). Place the stick guage against the canvas and hold it with your left hand. Carry the yarn over and under the gauge with your right hand (Figures C and D) and secure with a knot through the canvas (Figures E and F). The knot in Figures E and F is the same as in A and B. Continue working one knot at a time from left to right, beginning with the bottom row.

When the gauge stick is covered, cut the loops along the edge with a single-edge razor or very sharp embroidery scissors to release it. The Smyrna Knot should be worked on a frame or flat surface, not in the hand. It creates a velvet pile, and is ideal for geometric designs. For a shaggy, free-style effect, use the Turkish or Rya knots.

FIGURE 35
Smyrna Knot Stitch Detail

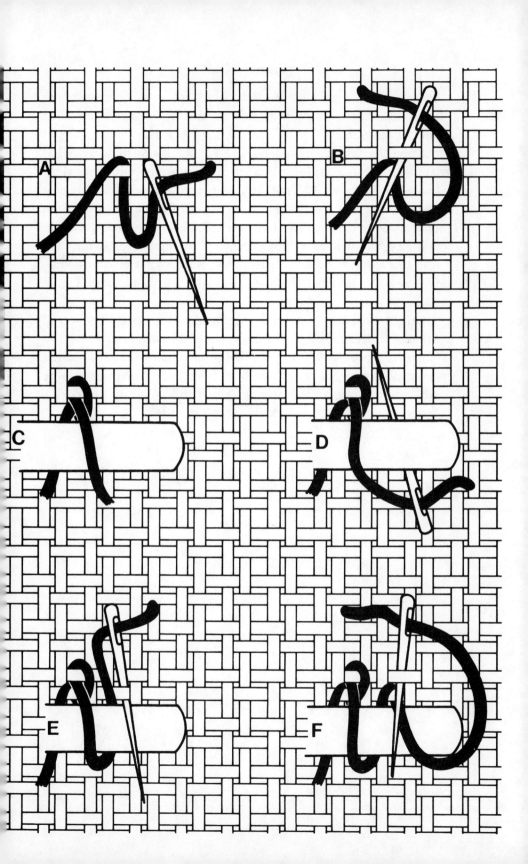

French Knots

French Knots may be used in clusters to create an interesting knubby texture or singly, to fill an area with lightly scattered dots. (Figure 36.)

Bring the threaded needle up at 1, hold the yarn in your left hand, and place the needle in a horizontal position with your right hand against point 1. Twist the yarn over and under the needle and, holding the yarn with the left hand, lift the needle into an upright position and insert it into the fabric one thread over at point 2. Pull the needle through slowly, and don't release the yarn held in the left hand until it is almost flush with the knot. When the knot is completed it should look like a little turban. (Figure 37.)

Do not twist yarn around the needle more than once. The size of the knot is determined by the thickness of the yarn used.

French Knots may be used to fill flower centers and seed pods or to simulate curly textures, such as lamb fur. Whenever a large stitch pattern has an open center, a French Knot will fit in attractively, especially when worked in shiny thread.

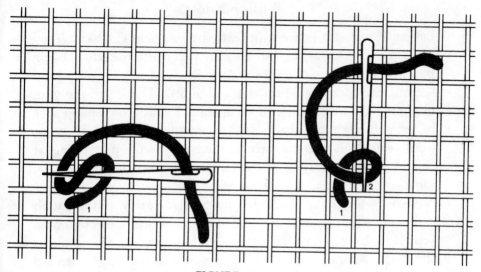

FIGURE 36
French Knot Stitch Detail

FIGURE 37
French Knots

Bullion Knots

Bullion Knots add interesting texture to creative stitchery. They may take a little practice, but they are well worth the effort. Begin by working with heavier yarn and needle. (Figure 38.)

Bring threaded needle up at 1 and in at 2. Don't pull the yarn through, but bring the needle up again at 1, this time coming only halfway through the fabric. Hold the needle underneath with one hand while twisting the yarn around the needle protruding at point 1. Twist tightly until the number of twists seem to be the same size as the space between 1 and 2.

Hold the top of the needle and the twisted yarn with the thumb and forefinger of your left hand, and draw the needle through with your right hand. Loosen the loops slightly to allow the needle to slip freely. As the needle passes through the coiled loops, the yarn at 2 is pulled under and the twisted coil lies flat between 1 and 2. Pull the yarn gently, as shown in Figure E, and insert needle at 2. If the stitches are not even at first, stroke them with the needle under the twist as you pull the yarn.

Keep bullion knots less then 1″ long. When you learn to work straight lines, work a row of looped bullion knots. Create the loops by adding an extra few twists around the needle so that the knot curves slightly instead of lying flat. (Figure 39.)

FIGURE 38
Bullion Knot Stitch Detail

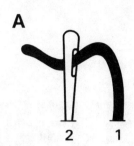

A

B

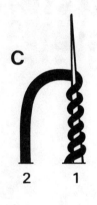

C

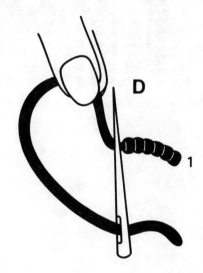

D

E

FIGURE 39
Bullion Knots

Beads and Sequins

(See color page 3.)

Beads and Sequins add interest and highlights to stitchery. Use sparingly between stitches or as a replacement for a stitch or two. (Figure 40.)

Sequins are worked individually. The needle comes out through the opening, a small bead is slipped through the needle, and the needle goes back into the same opening. The bead holds the sequin down. Beads can be applied singly or in clusters of four or five.

Purchase a small number of Beads and Sequins, a special beading needle, and thread, and practice with various fabrics and stitches. Fasten the working thread frequently on the reverse side of the fabric so that if it ever breaks, only a few beads or sequins will be lost.

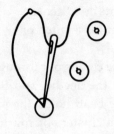
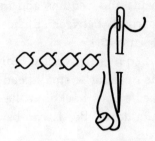

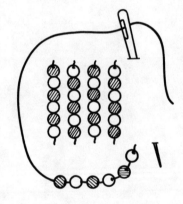

FIGURE 40
Applying Beads and Sequins (see color page 3, top)

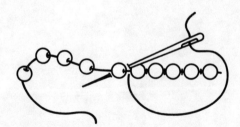

PROJECTS

Looped Flowers

(See color pages 1 and 4.)

Flowers made with Turkish Knots look three dimensional and may be finished in a variety of shapes and sizes. Use them in raised stitchery designs and to decorate large straw hats and pillows.

To make a flower with French Knot centers, draw four circles, one inside the other (use small glasses or boxtops for the outlines). Work a cluster of French Knots (page 62) with two-ply Persian-type yarn in yellow or light orange. Fill the center completely. Work a contrasting colored row of Turkish Knots (page 55) in 3/4" loops around each circle, beginning with the largest and ending with the smallest. (Figure 41.)

Cut out the flower around the outer circle of petals. Fold back the cut edge and stitch it to the underside.

There are many variations of this basic flower. Three are described below.

1. Instead of French Knot centers, work six small Turkish Knots in a pale yellow, single-ply yarn. Work the petal loops around the circles and vary the lengths slightly. (Figure 42.)

2. Fill the centers with several tight rows of Turkish Knots. After the petals are finished, cut the center loops evenly and brush them with a stiff nail brush. (Figure 43.)

3. Begin working the loops (Turkish Knots) in the center. Work them around in a pinwheel until the flower is at least 2" in diameter. Do not cut the loops. (Figure 44.)

Cut and fold back the margin on each flower. They are much easier to work with as individual units. When they are finished, arrange them on a selected background and fasten them with small stitches in matching threads.

For best results, use Persian-type wool yarn on a medium-weight soft fabric. If the flowers seem a little crushed, shake them out or brush lightly and they will regain their freshness.

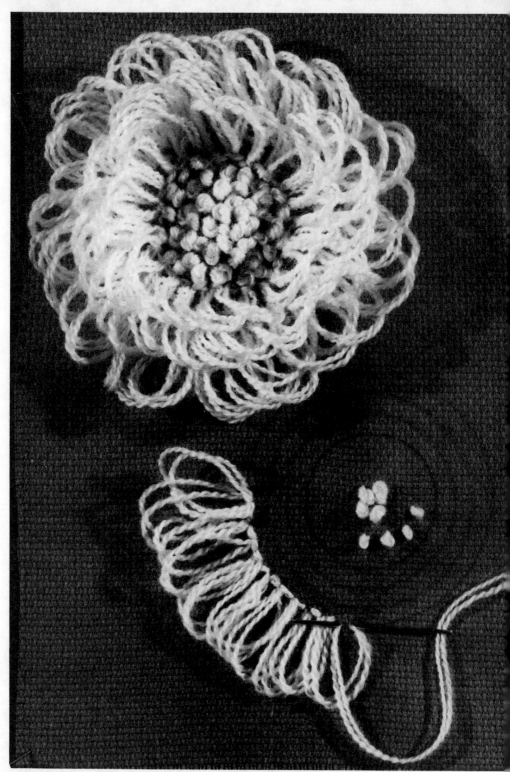

FIGURE 41 (See color pages 1 and 4)

FIGURE 42
(See color pages 1 and 4)

FIGURE 43
(See color pages 1 and 4)

FIGURE 44
(See color pages 1 and 4)

Red Rooster

(See color page 2.)

MATERIALS: 1 square # 18 mono canvas
1 oz. three-ply Persian-type yarn
(worked in single ply)

This design is worked entirely in the Buttonhole stitch from a counted-stitch graph. Each square is one unit and is translated into a series of seven Buttonhole stitches over seven canvas threads. (Figure 45.)

The design may be enlarged or reduced by altering the gauge of the *unit*. Canvas holes are not perfectly square, so five stitches worked over five canvas threads may not appear square. If this is the case, add or subtract one stitch, or extend or reduce the length of the stitch until the unit appears to be square. You may find that a unit of five stitches worked over four # 10 canvas threads is preferable to seven stitches over six # 18 canvas threads.

Once the gauge of canvas and number of stitches to the square unit have been established, measure the canvas. There are 54 units at the longest vertical line and 43 at the widest horizontal line. Multiply each unit by the number of stitches on the horizontal count and by the number of canvas threads on the vertical line. Allow 3" or 4" of space all around and an additional 3" for framing.

Draw two lines that cross over the center to divide the canvas into four quarters. The center point will coincide with the X in the center of the rooster. As you count the units, allow the appropriate number of stitches or canvas threads.

Begin at the bottom line of the leg and work upward, one line at a time, skipping over one or more units as indicated on the graph. Keep stitch lines as even as possible. End off yarn at the top of the stitch and come in with a new strand through the loop at the lower end to maintain an unbroken line.

Draw all lines with an ordinary # 2 graphite pencil. This will wash out with soap and warm water. Tapestry yarn of good quality will not run in warm water, and the canvas will not shrink perceptibly. Or have the article dry-cleaned. Be sure to machine stitch cut edges of canvas before washing to prevent raveling. Frame on canvas stretcher (see page 101).

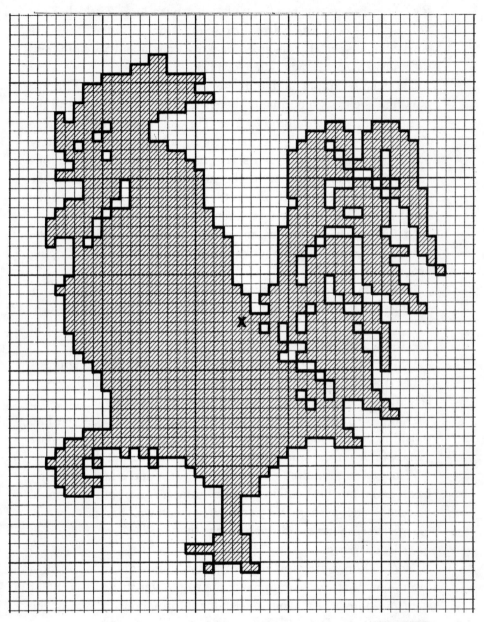

FIGURE 45
Red Rooster graph outline (see color page 2, Top)

Rya Rugs

Rya rugs are heavy needle-made rugs with long Turkish Knot stitches in heavy rug yarn. Originally from Sweden, they are worked on a specially designed backing known as Rya cloth, and the knots are sometimes called Rya Knots.

The small sample in Figure 46 illustrates a Rya rug in the making. The design outline is sketched with felt markers, and the colors are indicated lightly. The Turkish Knot Stitches (Rya Knots) are worked in horizontal rows from left to right, beginning at the bottom. The yarn colors are changed as needed within one row. At the color division line, the yarn is cut halfway through the loop and the tail end left on the top. The next loop begins in the same way as the first one (see stitch detail).

In the center of the design, a row of stitches illustrates the change in colors. This is only a sample. There is no skipping around in Rya work.

Rya cloth is easy to work on. The rows of open mesh are the right gauge for rug yarn or three full strands of Persian-type yarn. The rows of tightly woven fabric allow just the right amount of breathing space between the rows of stitches.

Pull the knots tightly, and work the loops in random lengths. When the rug is finished, clip and adjust the length of loops, leaving some uncut. There are no knots on the reverse side, and the rug does not require blocking or lining. The selvages need no finishing because they are covered by the loops. The cut edges are simply folded under and stitched securely with carpet thread.

A looped rug requires a great deal of yarn, and a large one may be an ambitious undertaking for a beginner. A first project should be a small one, perhaps a Rya pillow or small wall hanging.

Experiment with hand-dyed yarns; they look exceptionally well on large shag rugs.

Note: Do not attempt to piece a Rya rug. This is a job for a professional. If you plan to make the rug larger than the width of the cloth allows, ask your dealer for information on joining the cloth. Finished Turkish Knot rugs should be placed over a rug pad.

FIGURE 46 Turkish Knots on Rya Cloth

Embroidered Buttons

Special buttons that can be covered with your choice of fabric are available in notions and sewing supplies departments. They are easy to assemble and require no special tools. (Figure 47.)

Outline the circles in the appropriate size on a piece of cloth suitable for buttons. Embroider a simple design in the center of each circle. A double lazy daisy in contrasting thread, a tiny initial, or any small motif that is not too bulky works very well. Embroider all the buttons at one time. Cut out and cover according to the manufacturer's instructions.

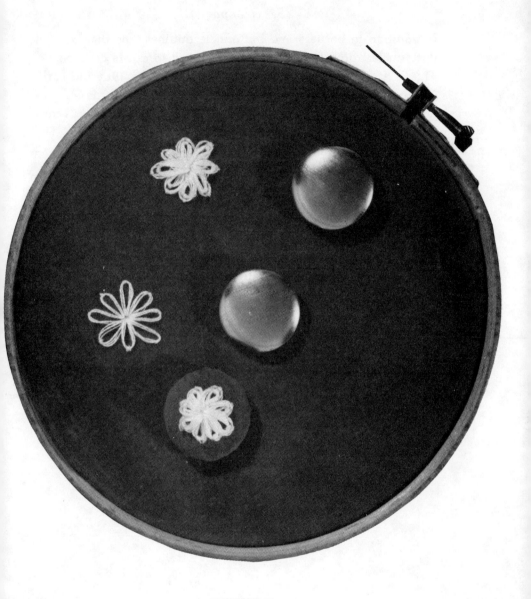

FIGURE 47

Card Boxes

(See color page 4.)

In addition to borders and buttonhole outlines, the Blanket and Buttonhole Stitch formations may be used to create card boxes. This is a charming craft that was popular in the 19th and early 20th centuries. A combination of thrift and artistry turns old picture postcards and greeting cards into decorative boxes. Each card is outlined with a border of Buttonhole or Blanket Stitches. The borders are then sewn together, edge-to-edge, to provide sharp-cornered, straight-sided boxes. (Figure 48.)

MATERIALS: Picture postcards, greeting cards, playing cards, or photographs
Six-strand embroidery floss, such as D.M.C. or Coats & Clark's

TOOLS: Tracing wheel with serrated edge
Small ruler
Sharp # 6 or # 7 needle with fairly long shaft

To make a small box from playing cards, you will need five cards. Cut one card into a square to be used as the base.

With tracing wheel and ruler, draw a sharp line around each card 1/4" from the edge. The tracing wheel will leave a dotted imprint that will serve as a guideline for the stitches. If the dots are not clearly visible, mark them with a fine-point pen in a color to match the thread (Figure 48, C).

Looped Flowers (Figures 41, 42, 43, and 44).

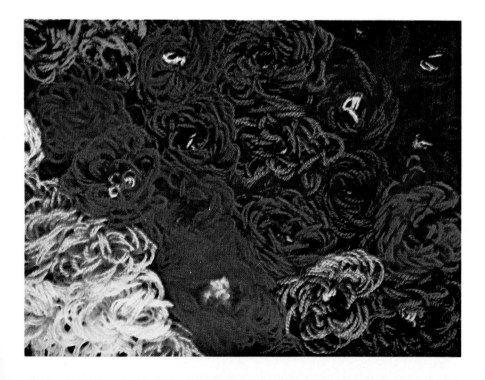

Top: Red Rooster (Figure 45).

Bottom: Chinese Butterflies and Flowers (Figures 52 and 53).

Top: Scarf (Figure 40 and Page 87).

Bottom: Aida Cloth worked with an assortment of stitches (Figures 54 and 55).

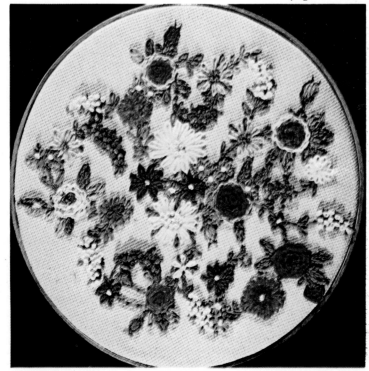

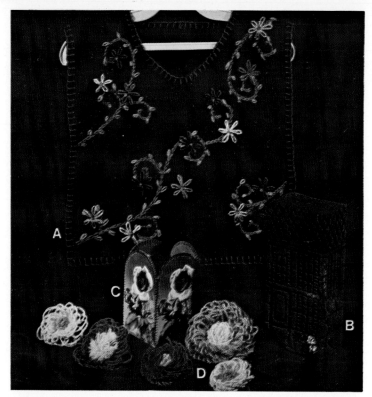

Top: A, Embroidered Tunic (Figure 59); B, Brick Cover (Figures 56, 57, and 58); C, Card Box (Figures 48, 49, 50, and 51); D, Looped Flowers (Figures 41, 42, 43, and 44).

Bottom: Pillow decorated with Looped Flowers (Figures 41, 42, 43, and 44).

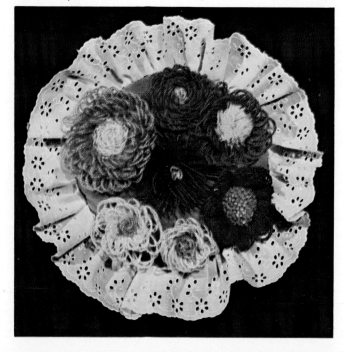

c   b   a

e   f

d

FIGURE 48

81

Thread the needle with two strands of the six-strand embroidery floss. Make a small knot and, beginning at the side of each card, work an even outline of Blanket or Buttonhole Stitches all around (Figure 49, A and B). Finish off the thread by twisting the last few stitches through the closed loops at the edge.

Fasten the four cards along the edges to form the walls of the box (Figure 49, C and D). Fasten the bottom square in the same manner (Figure 49, E). Check and clip all loose thread ends. Thinner cards such as photographs or greeting cards should be doubled to give the box stability. For each side, edge two cards with Buttonhole Stitches. Place them wrong side together and sew along the edges, catching the thread loops. Prepare each side, top, and bottom in this manner and assemble them as in Figure 49, C, D, and E.

To make a rounded cover (Figure 50), follow the instructions on page 80. Bend one card over the top of the finished box. Trace the curve outline on another card. You will need one card for the top dome, one card for the underside, and two semi-circles as outlined on page 84. Outline each piece in Buttonhole Stitches and sew them together as shown in Figure 49, page 83. Fasten one side of the boxtop to the base, using the same stitch technique. The box will open and close easily.

Boxes can be constructed in various shapes and sizes as shown in Figure 51.

FIGURE 49

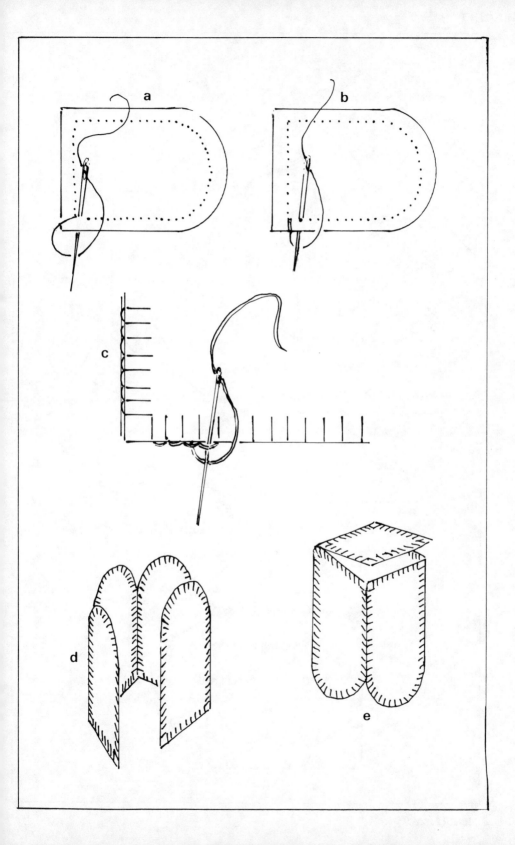

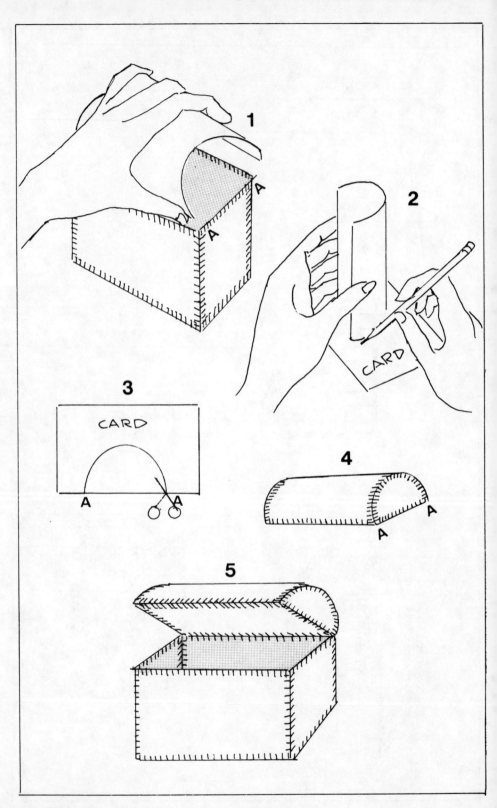

1

2

3

CARD

A   A

4

A
A

5

FIGURE 50

FIGURE 51
(See color page 4, Top, C)

Chinese Butterflies
and Flowers

(See color page 2.)

The diagram for this project is shown in actual size in Figures 52 and 53. Trace both parts on tracing paper and tape together at the dividing line A–B. Transfer with transfer paper or Hectograph (hot-iron pencil) according to the general instructions on page 13.

The design outline is worked in white silk thread on blue velveteen and stretched on an embroidery frame. Work with chain stitches, French Knots, and Fly Stitches or any combination of stitches. (This is a small design and may be worked in the hand instead of on a frame.)

Small Pillow

The diagram for this project is shown in actual size in Figures 54 and 55. Trace both parts on tracing paper and tape together at the dividing line A–B. Transfer according to general instructions on page 13. Embroider circles with rows of Chain Stitches; all lines are lazy daisies or detached Chain Stitches. The large and small dots are French Knots. Follow the color photograph on page C3, or choose your own color combination. Block and make into a small pillow following the finishing instructions on page 104.

Scarf

(See color page 3.)

Use any print scarf, and outline the scarf's design in Chain Stitches with cotton embroidery thread. Add a few sequins and beads for a jeweled effect. Beads and sequins should be worked on an embroidery frame. For bead and sequin placement, see diagram on page 68.

FIGURE 52-53
Actual-size diagram for Chinese Butterflies and Flowers (see color page 2, Bottom). Trace and align A-A, B-B for full pattern.

A|

FIGURE 54 - 55
Actual-size diagram for Flowers (see color page 3, Bottom)
Trace and align A–A, B–B for full pattern.

B|

Brick Cover

(See color page 4.)

Covered bricks make attractive bookends and paperweights. They can be covered with any type of embroidered fabric. Bricks vary in size and, because a brick cover should fit snugly, it is important to measure the dimensions of the brick before enlarging the design. (Figure 56.)

MATERIALS: One brick
Medium-weight fabric (any color)
Felt for lining
One skein black six-strand embroidery floss, plus a few strands in assorted colors
Sharp-pointed needle
Transferring materials (see general instructions)

Enlarge design to fit the brick and transfer it onto the fabric according to general instructions on page 13. Embroider all outlines in Chain Stitches. Use detached Chain Stitches on flowers and leaves. This is a very simple embroidery and should not be embellished.

To finish, wrap the brick with felt. Do not overlap felt. Cut a strip to wrap around the length, and stitch it at the edge. Cut another piece to fit around the width of the brick, and stitch it along all the edges. Felt should be taut on all sides (see diagram on page 94).

Press the embroidered cover and wrap it around the brick as if wrapping a package. The dotted lines should fit on the edges. Align the pattern lines as they meet around the brick, fold in the edges, and sew along the side with small stitches. (Figure 57.) Fold the fabric neatly over the top and bottom parts. Cut away any surplus fabric and stitch in place. The embroidered cover should also fit snugly around the brick. (Figure 58.)

Felt covered bricks make excellent weights for large needlework projects.

Note: Make sure the bricks are thoroughly dry before wrapping. Dry them in a low oven for about an hour, and let them cool completely before handling.

FIGURE 56
Diagram for Brick Cover (see color page 4, Top, B and Figure 58). Diagram is one-half actual size.

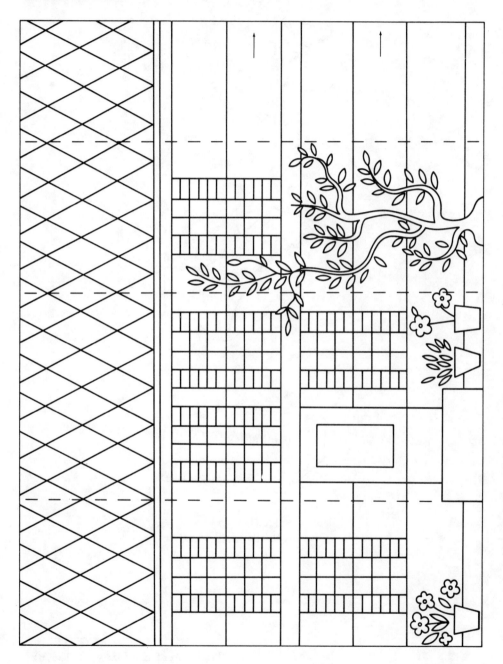

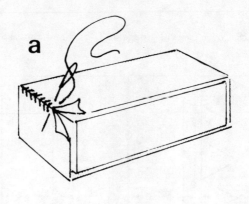

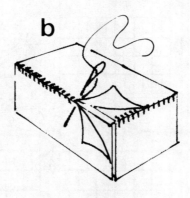

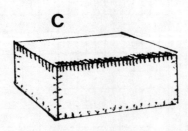

FIGURE 57
Covering Brick with felt lining

FIGURE 58
Finished Brick Cover (see color page 4, Top, B)

95

Embroidered Tunic

(See color page 4.)

Make a simple embroidered tunic in one afternoon. Use felt or any soft woolen fabric. You'll need one rectangle of fabric with an opening for the head. Measure the width across the shoulders and add any desired length.

Work a row of Blanket Stitches all around the cut edges. (Figure 59.) If the fabric tends to ravel, fold the edge once before stitching. Draw the design free-hand with a light marking pen or chalk pencil. Work stems in Chain stitches, leaves in detached Chain Stitches, and flowers in Lazy Daisy Stitch patterns.

FIGURE 59
Embroidered Tunic Diagram (see color page 4, Top, A)

Alphabet

The alphabet in Figures 60 and 61 has large, squared letters that will accomodate almost any type of stitchery. Outline them in Chain or Buttonhole Stitches and fill with French Knots or Lazy Daisies. Enlarge them to any size for free-style or counted-stitch embroidery.

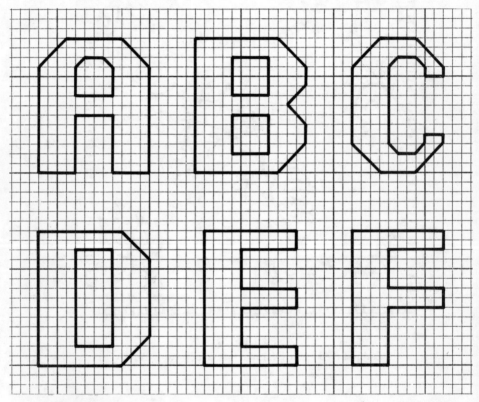

FIGURE 60
All-purpose Alphabet

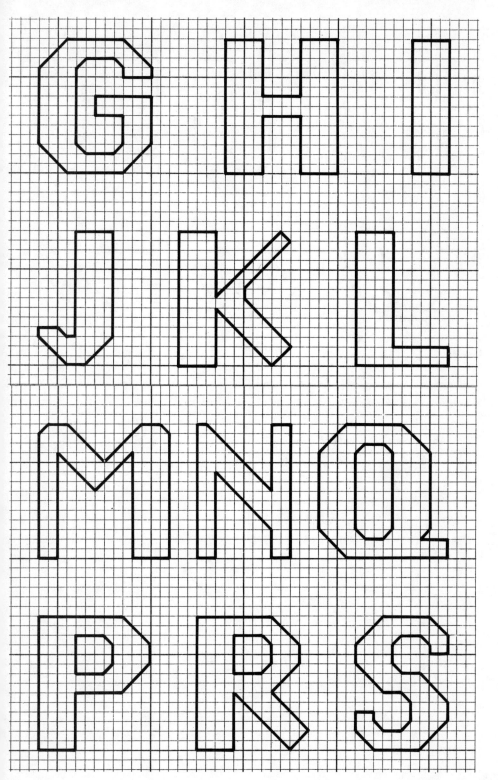

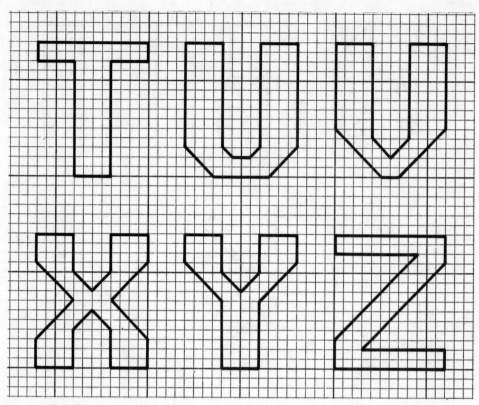

FIGURE 61
All-purpose Alphabet (W = inverted M)

XX

FINISHING INSTRUCTIONS

Blocking Textured Needlework

Textured stitches on soft fabrics have a tendency to pucker the fabric and make it appear wrinkled. A large project is normally worked on a frame, in which case it needs little or no blocking.

Any embroidery worked in the hand will have to be blocked. You will need a flat, smooth board, such as an old oak tabletop or a piece of composition board. Do not use plywood, veneered wood, or any warped surface. The board should be somewhat larger than the needlework.

Wet the fabric lightly with a spray mist of water. Mist the wrong side and turn it over to block right-side *up*. Stretch and pull the fabric gently but firmly, placing push pins all around the worked area. The fabric should be smooth and wrinkle-free and the weave of the threads very straight. As the fabric is stretched, the stitches will lift and fluff out. Let the piece dry at room temperature, and then remove it from the board. This method is more satisfactory than steam ironing, which tends to pucker the fabric around the heavier stitches.

Framing Needlework

A piece of needlework cannot be framed like a photograph or a poster, nor should it be glued to a board. For best results it must be stretched on a frame.

The best frame for needlework is the simple, sturdy artist's frame. These frames are sold in individual strips of 6" and up. Each end of the strip is grooved and mitered for easy assembly.

After needlework has been stretched on an artist's frame, it can be slipped into a decorative frame. Decorative frames are sold in packages of pre-finished strips of one length. Since frame sizes are precut, check the supply of ready-made frames in your area before deciding on the design and dimensions of your needlework.

Once the frames have been selected, finish and block the needlepoint. Assemble the artist's frame, steam the needlepoint to relax canvas (see blocking information on page 101), and place it over the frame. The worked area should not extend over the edge of the frame.

Place a few push pins into the corners and around the sides to keep the canvas from shifting. Fold the unworked margin of canvas over the edge of the frame, and staple the center point on each side of the frame. The rows of stitches should look straight and the needlework smooth and even. Be careful not to overstretch.

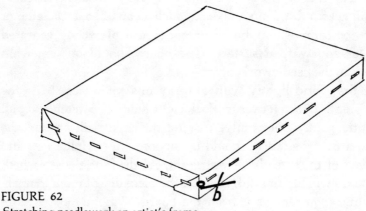

FIGURE 62
Stretching needlework on artist's frame

Staple all around the frame, folding corners neatly as shown in Figure 62. If the staples protrude slightly, hammer them in. If a professional stapler is not available, use carpet tacks 1/4" apart.

Cut the canvas along the edges and place the finished piece in a decorative frame. Do not place glass over needlework unless you are framing a fragile antique; and in that case, have a professional do the job. Antique frames can be used for needlework if they are deep enough to accommodate the artist's frame. A frame that was used for an oil painting is more suitable than one used for a photograph. Custom frames should always be handled by a professional.

Note: The edge of the decorative frame should cover one or two rows of stitched canvas all around. Allow for this in the preliminary planning of the needlepoint.

Mitering Fabric

For neatly folded corners, learn to miter fabric rectangles and squares. Indicate a center outline with pencil or basting line. If a design is embroidered in the center, this can serve as the outline.

Clip the corners and fold to the inner outline. Fold over lateral sides until they meet on the diagonal miter line. Baste all around and sew with small stitches. Remove bastings and press work if necessary. (Figure 63.)

FIGURE 63
Mitering fabric

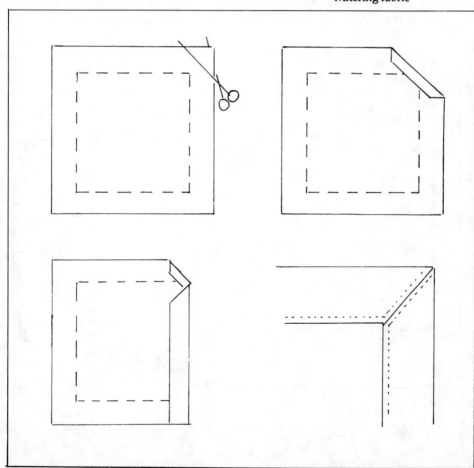

How to Make a Pillow

The loveliest pillows are usually the simplest to make. They show off the stitchery with a minimum of frills and ruffles. (Figure 64.)

MATERIALS: Fabric backing in the same size and approximate weight as the needlework (velvet, duck, upholstery fabric, etc.)
Pillow filler, 1" larger than dimension of needlework (choose dacron polyester or feathers and down—both are available ready-made in department stores.)
Decorative twisted cord or braid (optional)

Press fabric and pin to blocked needlework with right sides together. Stitch several rows of large basting (running) stitches across the entire width of the two fabrics at 2" intervals. These basting stitches will keep both fabrics flat and even.

Remove pins, and machine stitch on the needlepoint side as indicated in diagram outline. Two rows of large machine stitches sewn at the widest setting are better than one row of little stitches.

Clip corners at points and remove basting threads. Turn pillow right-side out. Poke out the corners with your fingers.

FIGURE 64
How to Make a Pillow

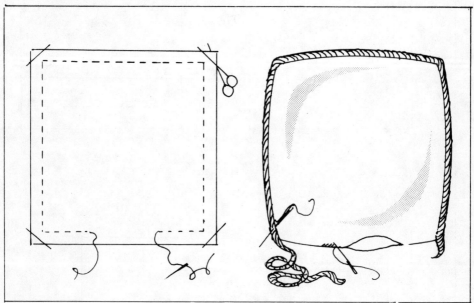

Measure the entire outline of the pillow and cut a length of cord or braid one inch longer. Don't stretch the cord while measuring. Tie a piece of thread close to the cut edges to prevent the cord from separating.

Beginning at the open end, pin the cord along the edge of the pillow to cover the machine stitching. Take small stitches in matching thread, and stop at the other end of the pillow opening. Secure the cord at that point with an extra stitch and remove needle. Finish stitching the cord after the pillow is stuffed.

To stuff pillow, push a cotton ball into each corner, and then insert the pillow filler. Fold the filler in half, slip it into the opening, and unfold it inside the casing. Hand stitch the opening closed by folding the needlework and fabric into the opening and lining up the edges with the existing machine stitching.

Re-thread needle on decorative cord and stitch it over the closed edge. Overlap the end pieces of the cord and tie the remaining thread over the two to keep them from unraveling. End with a few stitches.

Note: The opening and the ends of the decorative cord should be placed at the bottom of the pillow. Check the needlepoint design before basting the outline.

XX

LIST OF SUPPLIERS

Retail Only

La Stitcherie
72 Middle Neck Road
Great Neck, New York 11021

Canvas, yarn, kits, custom designs

Wholesale and Retail

Toni Toes of Vermont, Inc.
Route 100
South Londonderry, Vermont 05155

Handbags, kits for tennis racquet covers, belts for needlepoint, plastic enclosures
Will send catalogue

Walbead, Inc.
38 West 37th Street
New York, New York 10018

Beads, sequins, macrame
Will send catalogue

Wholesale Only

Paternayan Brothers, Inc.
312 East 95th Street
New York, New York 10028

Paternayan Persian yarn, canvas and needles, rug and crewel yarns, Rya cloth

Craft Yarns of Rhode Island
P.O. Box 151
Harrisville, R.I.

Three-ply Persian-type yarn, quick-point yarn, needlepoint canvas

Coats and Clark's
P.O. Box 1966
Stamford, Connecticut 06904

Cotton and rayon embroidery threads and rug yarns, craft yarns (acrylic washable), acrylic Persian-type yarn, needles

Handwork Tapestries
114 B Allen Blvd.
Farmingdale, New York 11735

Persian-type yarn, Laine Colbert three-ply tapestry yarn, Colbert six, French silk, canvas

Art Needlework Treasure Trove P.O. Box 2440 Grand Central Station New York, New York 10017	Canvas, yarns, linens, embroidery fabrics, and supplies
Howard Needlework Supply Co., Inc. 919 Third Avenue New York, New York 10022	Canvas and embroidery fabric in linen, cotton, and polyester
William E. Wright Co. One Penn Plaza New York, New York 10001	Lace
E.T. Group Ltd. 230 Fifth Avenue New York, New York 10017	Paternayan yarns, Alice Peterson painted canvases, Rya cloth
George Wells The Ruggery Cedar Swamp Road Glen Head, New York 11545	Rug yarns, linen and Rya cloth, undyed yarn, special dyes for wool yarns, Hectograph pencils
Astor Place Ltd. 260 Main Avenue Stirling, New Jersey 07980	Painted canvases and packaged kits
Cute and Custom 1A Munson Court Melville, New York 11746	Painted canvases and packaged kits
Needlepoint U.S.A. 37 West 57th Street New York, New York 10019	Painted canvases and packaged kits

Note: For all inquiries to dealers, enclose a self-addressed stamped envelope.

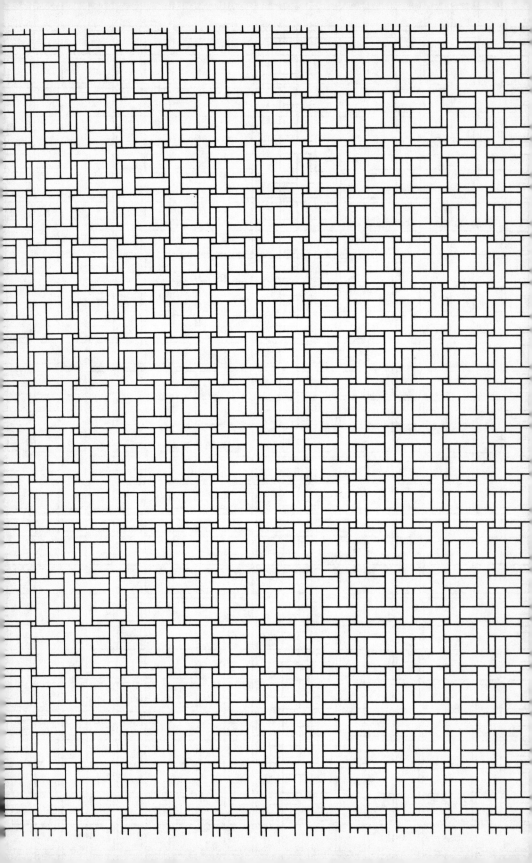

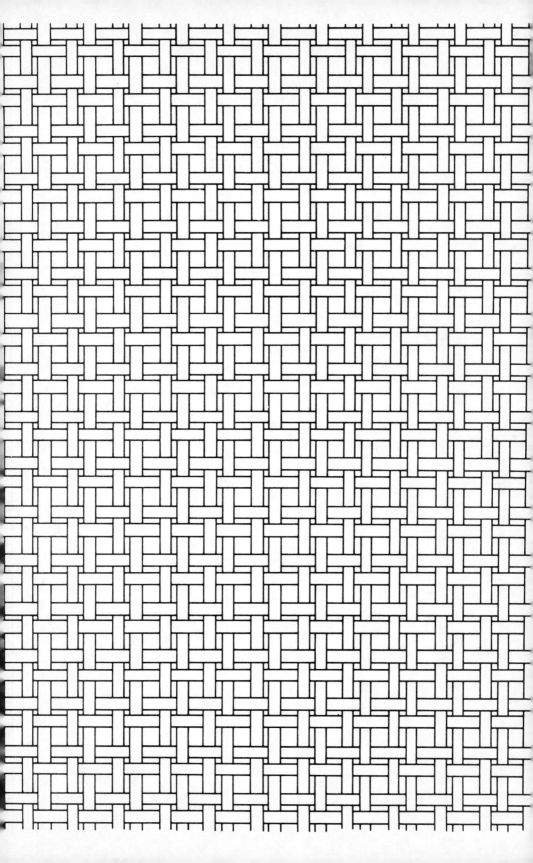